ADVANCE PRAISE

"Brian Scudamore's enthralling tale of the launch and longevity of 1-800-GOT-JUNK? is everything you want from a business yarn. Toxic employees, poor decisions, and financial and personal loss can't dim the persistence and optimism of an entrepreneur who transformed the simplest of ideas into a $250M-plus multi-brand empire. This book will make you want to run—arms flung wide—toward entrepreneurship."

LEIGH BUCHANAN, EDITOR AT
LARGE AT *INC. MAGAZINE*

"It's no surprise that Brian Scudamore has experienced the incredible highs and lows of entrepreneurship; he's been in the battle for 30 years! In WTF?! (Willing to Fail), he bares it all—the good, the bad, and the ugly—in a way that will help entrepreneurs on their own journey. If I had to sum this book up, I'd say,

'Learn from Brian's mistakes so you don't have to!' We should all be open to learning from those who have done it before!"

JOE DE SENA, CEO AND FOUNDER OF SPARTAN RACE, *NEW YORK TIMES* BEST-SELLING AUTHOR, AND WORLD-CLASS ENDURANCE ATHLETE

"Brian Scudamore is one of the hidden gems of the entrepreneurial world. In this book, he conveys life lessons with humility and wisdom. With a healthy dose of fun and entertainment (and blue wigs), Brian delves into counterintuitive insights about commitment vs. passion, work vs. play, and the turning points in life that shaped him, not only describing the key lessons he's learned but also the events that triggered those lessons."

DR. NOAM WASSERMAN, FOUNDING DIRECTOR OF FOUNDER CENTRAL, USC, AND AUTHOR OF THE BEST-SELLING *THE FOUNDER'S DILEMMAS*

"In this very readable book, culled from 30-years' experience, Brian Scudamore details how budding entrepreneurs must be WTF (Willing to Fail) if they hope to truly succeed. Highly recommended."

JUSTIN MARTIN, AUTHOR AND ONE-TIME WRITER FOR *FORTUNE* MAGAZINE

"Brian Scudamore's story is both improbable and inspiring. From a chance 'lightbulb' moment at a McDonald's to the purchase of a $700 beat-up truck... Brian built a billion-dollar brand with his own two hands. Was he lucky? You bet. Was his timing right? Yes. But he also busted his butt to build an elegant and simple business that went on to spawn competitors and rivals. 1-800-GOT-JUNK? is a story full of failure, struggle, crisis and ultimately success through grit. And Brian lived that story."

GUY RAZ, HOST OF NPR'S *HOW I BUILT THIS*

"The best learning comes from those who 'have done it', and Brian Scudamore sure has. WTF?! is not only a fun and easy read, but I pulled 15 business and life takeaways that will enhance my life and the lives of the CEOs I coach on a monthly basis."

JACK DALY, MULTIPLE BEST-SELLING AUTHOR ON AMAZON AND CEO COACH

"When an accomplished person like Brian opens up about his failures as much as his successes, the lessons are powerful. This book is worth more than an MBA."

PAT LENCIONI, BEST-SELLING AUTHOR OF *THE FIVE DYSFUNCTIONS OF A TEAM*, BUSINESS CONSULTANT, AND SPEAKER

"Brian Scudamore is everyman's entrepreneur, taking ordinary companies and converting them into exceptional companies, then spreading them worldwide. This book tells the story of how everyone can, with great, productive joy, literally transform the world!"

MICHAEL E. GERBER, AUTHOR OF *THE E-MYTH* BOOKS

"Clear, candid, and fun to read, Brian Scudamore's book is a great crash course for anyone who wants to start and scale a business."

ELAINE POFELDT, AUTHOR OF *THE MILLION-DOLLAR, ONE-PERSON BUSINESS*

"Brian Scudamore has taken ordinary service businesses and turned them into exceptional customer service experiences—four times over. He truly understands how to scale businesses and has turned his WTF attitude into a recipe for massive growth. This book is an essential tool for anyone taking on the adventure of entrepreneurship."

VERNE HARNISH, FOUNDER, ENTREPRENEURS' ORGANIZATION, AND AUTHOR OF *SCALING UP (ROCKEFELLER HABITS 2.0)*

"It's not easy to turn one business into a multi-million-dollar success, and Brian Scudamore's done it four times. In his first book, he opens up about how he transformed a single junk truck into a home-services empire, and how if he can do it—anyone can. This is a must-read for anyone looking for guidance on their entrepreneurial journey."

ROBERT HERJAVEC, CELEBRITY ENTREPRENEUR ON *SHARK TANK* AND *DRAGON'S DEN* AND CEO OF HERJAVEC GROUP

"Success in entrepreneurship really comes down to attitude, and Brian Scudamore proves he's got the right one. In his first book, he shares how he's learned to transform failure into learning opportunities, how finding amazing people and treating them well is the key to growth, and that business should be fun. His "WTF" philosophy is a secret weapon for anyone looking to scale their business, create great culture, and turn challenges into triumphs."

JJ RAMBERG, HOST OF MSNBC'S *YOUR BUSINESS* AND COFOUNDER OF GOODSHOP.COM

"*Success is all about attitude. With its upbeat, positive tone, this book is an essential tool for anyone looking for guidance as they take on the adventure of entrepreneurship.*"

TONY HSIEH, CEO OF ZAPPOS AND *NEW YORK TIMES* BEST-SELLING AUTHOR OF *DELIVERING HAPPINESS*

WTF?! (WILLING TO FAIL)

WTF?!
WILLING TO FAIL

HOW FAILURE CAN BE
YOUR KEY TO SUCCESS

BRIAN SCUDAMORE

WITH ROY H. WILLIAMS

LIONCREST

PUBLISHING

WTF?! (WILLING TO FAIL)

How Failure Can Be Your Key to Success

ISBN   978-1-5445-0108-6 *Hardcover*

        978-1-5445-0107-9 *Ebook*

For Grandpa Kenny and Grandma Florence
who first lit my entrepreneurial fire.

CONTENTS

INTRODUCTION

I wrote this book to encourage you.

I'm the most ordinary guy there is. I didn't start a tech company or invent an app. I don't party with rock stars or drive a fancy car. My colleagues, friends, and family will tell you, "Brian is a regular guy."

After nearly thirty years, my little junk hauling company is doing an average of a million dollars a day, and I see a clear pathway to becoming a billion-dollar company. You can do something big, too, if you want. But you've got to be willing to fail.

Failure is a temporary condition.

Afterward, it is a lesson learned.

It is wisdom gained.

I've experienced moments of triumph and felt fulfillment that, in the beginning, I never could have imagined. But these moments have been punctuated by challenges I've faced, mistakes I've made, and failures I've endured.

I'm going to share all these with you so you can learn from my mistakes. After all, why should both of us have to learn the same hard lessons the hard way?

I've been lucky to be surrounded by passionate, hardworking people I can count on, people who want to build something bigger and better—together.

The best parts of your life, the moments you'll remember forever, will happen because of the awesome people standing next to you.

I didn't do it alone, and you can't either.

Do you want to go on an adventure of entrepreneurship?

Do you want to take the road less traveled?

Do you want to begin your own founder's story?

If I can do it, so can you.

—Brian

DIFFICULTIES AND SECRET GETAWAYS

I got a dad when I was seven.

Charles Scudamore was studying to become a doctor, and lucky for me, he fell in love with my mother.

"I do."

"I do."

"And I'm with her. It's sort of a package deal. Hi, my name is Brian."

Then, whoosh!—Charles Scudamore whisked Mom and me from our home in San Francisco to Vancouver, which is in a whole other country.

So now I'm a foreigner, a seven-year-old American in Canada, and the only thing I cared about—the only thing I really wanted—was to fit in, to belong, to have friends.

My problem was I tried too hard. I became the class clown, always making fun of other kids in an attempt to get a laugh, get noticed, be accepted. I became an expert at pushing people's buttons and yanking their chains.

I hope you never did that. If you did, I'm sure you learned the same thing I learned: *those other kids just wanted to be accepted, too.* And my teasing was making them feel rejected.

It took me six long years to figure out that making other people feel bad wasn't the best way to make them want to hang out with you.

Here's how I survived those lonely years of being the class clown, the disruptor, the troublemaker: I went home during recess. Our house was a stone's throw from the school, so I'd always be quick out the door, then run to my house and sit alone until I heard the bell that signaled the end of recess. I'd watch out the window until everyone who wanted to kick my butt had gone back inside, then I'd sprint to school and rejoin the class.

Getting home at the end of the school day was a little trickier. I got beat up a lot until I discovered a secret getaway. When the other kids were walking toward the school exit, I'd walk in the other direction to the school library. Then, when no one was looking, I'd slip out the emergency exit door, which was almost directly across from my house.

Secret getaways require a lot of work (even the happy, healthy kind): cooking, skiing, traveling, learning a new language, being a mentor, being a coach, playing with kids—you get the picture.

If you don't have a happy, healthy secret getaway—or better yet, a few of them—you need to fling yourself into something. Don't wait until you miraculously discover you have a "passion" for this or that. Just pick something. Commit to it. And passion for it will follow.

Commitment leads to passion.

Passion does not lead to commitment.

I hope you never had to learn the painful lesson that rejecting other people leads only to unhappiness for both you and them. And if you did have to learn that awful lesson, I hope it didn't take you as long to figure it out.

It never occurred to my younger self that I had other self-possibilities. I had set a course for myself as the class clown and I was stuck there, like a train on tracks, plunging headlong into a dark, echoing tunnel of loneliness.

I'm still a prankster and a practical joker, but these days I'm careful not to make people feel bad. My jokes are never at someone else's expense.

When I got older, I learned that making fun of other people isn't the only way to make them feel bad. Constant moaning and complaining to them about your job, your boss, your lack of money, your inability to get a date, and the overall unfairness of life...well, that kind of talk bums people out, too.

But that's a subject for another chapter.

THE NEW KID—AGAIN

When I was twelve, Dad had to go to England to further his education as a liver transplant surgeon. He took us with him, of course.

I was looking forward to escaping my tormentors.

Problem: I was a bucktooth Canadian kid with shiny metal braces and a really bad haircut. Seriously, it looked like the barber put a bowl on my head and then shaved everything around the bowl.

To make matters worse, the whole time I was in England, I never saw another kid wearing braces.

And there was a popular TV show about a robot called *Metal Mickey*. You can see where this is headed, right?

First day of school. Recess. I'm on the playground, anxious for a fresh start, hoping never again to be the rejected kid, when a boy named Mike walks over to me, shoves my shoulder, and says, "Go back where you came from, Metal Mickey."

When I heard the other kids laughing, my right hand leapt up and out like it had a mind of its own.

As I stood there looking down at Mike, flat on his back, I'm not sure which of us was more surprised.

I did the wrong thing. Absolutely the wrong thing. And I still feel bad about it. I'm not a violent person.

But strangely, it worked out.

Did you ever do the wrong thing, then have it miraculously work to your advantage?

Mike was known as the class bully—the toughest kid in the school.

And I was the new kid who decked him.

Kids that had never noticed me suddenly saw me as a person. And some of them even wanted to talk to me! I went from being an outsider to being a protector in a single day.

But my new reputation came at a price. It wasn't long before another boy tried to beat me up, just to prove he could do it.

The English, as you know, are famously civilized. For a schoolchild to be "caned" is extremely rare in that country. So, to be the new kid who decked two school bullies *and endured a caning for it* made me something of a legend.

Fortunately, I was never tempted to hit anyone again.

And even more fortunately, I never had to.

I knew I didn't want to be a physical bully, but it had taken me half of my twelve-year-old life to learn that making fun of people was the wrong way to make friends. People are wounded by hurtful words just as quickly, and sometimes more deeply, than they are wounded by fists.

Things in England weren't perfect for me. I was still the dorky Canadian kid with the bad haircut, but I walked with my head held higher and my shoulders back. I had people who called me their friend.

But we weren't going to be in England forever.

Sooner or later, I'd be back in Vancouver.

And in Vancouver, they knew a whole different Brian.

Before I go any further, I'd like to make it clear that I'm aware you've lived a lot of these same experiences and learned most of these same lessons. In fact, you probably learned them quicker and better than I did.

But sometimes it's good to be reminded of what we've always known.

Sometimes it's good to remember.

BACK WHERE WE STARTED... BUT DIFFERENT

San Francisco to Vancouver to England to...Hong Kong?

"Or you can go back to Vancouver and live with your grandmother."

The only thing that frightened me more than moving back to Vancouver was being the new kid in a country where I didn't even know how to say hello.

"Hello, Grandma."

"Oh, Brian, it's so wonderful to see you! I love you so much." And then she smothered me with a big "grandmother hug."

After the hug, she held me in both of her hands at arm's length and smiled as she said, "Bri, we need to get you some new clothes and a haircut."

Grandma Scudamore was a life changer.

I'm betting you've had a person like that in your life—someone who liked you just for who you were, not for anything you had done. Someone who cared enough to help you get past your blind spot.

I looked and felt like a whole different kid when we walked out of that barber shop. The image I saw of myself in the mirror overturned the image I had of myself in my mind.

Self-image is a powerful thing.

Needless to say, the kids at school met a whole different Brian than the one who had left Vancouver a year and a half ago. Luckily, I had accumulated just enough wisdom during those eighteen months to play it soft and easy. Shoulders back, head high, this "new and improved" Brian spoke with a bit of a British accent and was easier to be around than the smart-mouthed, frightened, hurting Brian who fled this town eighteen months earlier.

Circumstances did some of the work for me. I'm not sure who I would have become in England if I had let Mike push me around on the playground.

And my new friends in England altered my self-image as well. I learned during my time with them how important it is for people to feel safe, how to encourage them and make them feel special.

But it was my grandmother who put the icing on my cake. She saw me as I really was and loved me anyway. Ida Scudamore helped me get past my blind spot.

I will forever be grateful for my grandmother's love and support. She helped me step out of an awkward, insecure phase when I only felt sorry for myself. Now, I take gratitude with me every-where I go, and it guides me in every aspect of my life. And it all started because my grandmother showed me compassion.

Gratitude has the power to change your life.

Has anyone ever helped you? A teacher? A coach? A neighbor? A friend of the family? A social worker? Think of the people who cared enough about you to help you when you couldn't help yourself. They saw you as you really were, and liked you anyway.

Are any of those people still around and able to be reached so you can look into their eyes and say, "Thank you"?

If they are, you're lucky to still have that chance.

DOUBLE DROPOUT

Whenever I'd get money for Christmas, Dad would say, "You need to write thank-you letters to those nice people and tell them you're saving that money for university."

But I wasn't saving it for university. I was spending it on experiences. I was using it to buy boxes of candy and sell the candy from my dorm room at a massive profit. I was investing in rare hockey cards and selling them at a premium.

Do you remember "The Road Not Taken" by Robert Frost? If so, you'll remember the ending:

I shall be telling this with a sigh.

Somewhere ages and ages hence:

Two roads diverged in a wood, and I—

I took the one less traveled by,

And that has made all the difference.

Do you enjoy taking the road less traveled? Me, too.

One of my roads less traveled is that I didn't graduate high school. I finished grade twelve, but I didn't graduate. It was a moment that took me by surprise.

Here's what happened. Instead of throwing a massive graduation party with a DJ and so on, the committee at our school decided to rent a beautiful old-school music hall, the Orpheum, where everyone would walk across the stage with poise and style and grace, our backs elegantly arched and our proud chins held high, radiating refinement and quality.

Whatever.

So I showed up in my suit and walked. But when I opened up the scroll they gave me, it was just a recognition that I had finished grade twelve. It didn't say that I graduated, only that I had attended.

I remember thinking for a moment that it was kind of cool. "Okay, here's a 'road less traveled' moment to remember: I'm the only one who didn't graduate!" But then it hit me that all my friends *had* graduated. They were going to university, and I wasn't.

I felt left out, just like I did in elementary school.

But then the older, wiser me showed up and said, "The reason you didn't graduate is because you skipped school and went out and drank with your buddies. You might have taken the road less traveled, but it wasn't a good one."

Have you ever taken a road that wasn't a good one? Of course you have. Hindsight is 20/20, but foresight is 50/50. Looking back, we can see with perfect clarity. But when we're at the crossroads looking forward, both ways look equally appealing.

Have you ever noticed that the really hard choices in life are when we have to choose between two good things? Freedom is a good thing, and responsibility is a good thing. And they often appear as equally attractive paths when we come to a fork in the road. In the past, I had always chosen freedom.

The older, wiser me decided to do the responsible thing. I was going to figure out how to go to university, even though I didn't have a high school diploma or money to pay for tuition.

Step One: I went to the admissions office and said, "Listen, I know I'm one class short, but I can do this. I'm smart enough. Please give me a chance."

Bingo. I'm in.

Step Two: I saw how to pay for my education when I noticed an old pickup truck ahead of me in the drive-thru line at McDonald's. Spray-painted on the sides of that truck were the words "Mark's

Hauling" and a phone number. I said to myself, "I could do that."

My plan was to work hard hauling junk and make enough money to pay for a year of college. It was a simple plan. Nothing special.

And then my truck broke down, two weeks in. I'd been full of adrenaline and excitement at the prospect of owning my own business, and getting a massive bill for repairs I couldn't afford almost took the wind out of my sails. In a lot of ways, it was my first real test as an entrepreneur, a chance to bounce back and stick to my plan. So I sucked up the unexpected cost and got things rolling again.

I couldn't afford to buy advertising from the sales department, so I decided to get some free press from the news department.

My girlfriend Lisa said, "Here's an angle: You couldn't find a summer job, so you created your own."

I said, "Cool." Then I looked in the phone book

and called the news desk of the *Vancouver Province*, one of the biggest papers in town. I said, "I've got an awesome story for you!"

They said, "Okay. What is it?" Intrigued by my enthusiasm, they listened.

I said, "I found out that it's a tight summer job market out there, so I created my own. I started a junk-removal business, The Rubbish Boys. Our phone number is 738-JUNK. And things are going *great*!"

They said, "Congratulations!" and sent out a reporter and a photographer. The next day, we were on the front page!

I was suddenly a rock star. The phone never quit ringing. Bus drivers would see us and wave that front page out the window when we drove past. My world changed in an instant, at the snap of a finger, and it changed for the better.

I still keep that front-page story on the wall in our office.

A few months later, I left the junior college that had accepted me because I really couldn't stand it. I was in the wrong place, and I knew it.

With an itch to experience the rest of Canada and the cultural diversity of Quebec, I traveled to Montreal, went to two different schools there, and performed really well.

Now I was able to come back to Vancouver and attend the University of British Columbia, which was really hard to get into. "Okay, now I have arrived. I can complete my degree here, and everything will be straightened out."

I had attended four schools in four years, all funded by hauling junk each summer in a rusty old Ford pickup truck that I bought with my life savings of $700.

It's important, I think, to be able to turn your work into play.

I remembered this one day when I got a call to haul off a mountain of escargot shells from an escargot import company that had gone bankrupt.

We loaded the truck to the brim, but the customer said to me, "Come on, guys, you can fit more in there than that."

The customer is always right. So we backed the truck up next to the building, ran up the stairs, and jumped out a second-floor window into the back of that truck. It was like landing in a huge pile of leaves. We ran up those stairs and dove out the window yelling, "Woo-hoo!" over and over until we were breathless with laughter. We were able to load a ton more escargot shells, we had fun, and the customer was really happy.

That was my life. And life was good.

So, every day before classes at the University of British Columbia, I would talk to customers, schedule their junk removal, chat with my employees, solve their problems, then drive across town to get educated.

The truth was, I was learning more about business by running one than I was learning by studying textbooks and attending classes. The first of a series of aha moments occurred in Organizational

Behavior class when the professor approached me and said, "I know you're running this business, The Rubbish Boys. I'd love to have you present to the class."

All my professors knew I was running a business, not because I told them, but because I carried a big Motorola cell phone that was about the size of a loaf of bread and heavier than a cement block. No vibrate function, no mute function. Occasionally, it would ring while I was in class, and I'd have to run out of the room to answer it because the friend I had hired to take care of things while I was at school wasn't always up to the job. I'd apologize to the professor after class and explain why the phone and the interruptions were necessary. They all seemed to feel a certain sympathy for me. I think they might have even been a little bit proud that one of their students was working his butt off so he could attend their class.

I delivered my presentation to the Organizational Behavior class, answered a ton of questions, and got a lot of enthusiastic feedback from people who loved hearing my start-up story and were energized by the challenges I was facing. That's when a voice in my head said, "I'm not really learning a lot here. In fact, I'm the guy teaching the lesson."

This was in 1993.

I sat down with my father and tried doing what I had done with the newspaper reporter. I said, "Dad, I got some good news for you." Trying to present my decision in a positive light, I said with a beaming smile, "I'm dropping out of university."

He sat there quietly for a moment, looking mildly confused, then said, "To be a full-time junk man?" I nodded confidently. He shook his head slowly and whispered, "You gotta be kidding me."

Here's my dad, a successful liver transplant surgeon who put himself through university by swinging a hammer on a series of construction jobs. He never blinked, never wavered. Dad crossed the finish line and rang the bell.

Here's me, dropping my education to go make a few dollars, learn by experience, and have an adventure.

"My oldest son is dropping out of university to become a full-time junk man? Where did I go wrong?"

CHAPTER 5

AFTER GRADUATION

Although I didn't graduate high school or university, I like to believe I graduated *magna cum laude* from The School of Consequences.

The final exam from that school is a single question: "What's the difference between confidence and hubris?"

The answer: "The outcome. If it turns out well, people will say you were bold and daring. You had confidence. But if it turns out to be a disaster, they'll say you were full of yourself and you're paying the price for your hubris."

My diploma from The School of Consequences is imaginary, but the school is real.

I was the class disruptor when I was a kid, and that didn't work out well until after I grew up.

Today, it's good to be a disruptor.

I disrupted the business of junk hauling with professionalism and customer service and turned it into a career that a person could be proud of. But it wasn't an easy thing to do.

Occasionally, I took the wrong fork in the road, then had to backtrack and take the other fork.

Has anyone ever told you that you can't go backward? They've told me that, too. I think I know what they're trying to say, but in my experience, an essential part of learning through consequences is that you're able to backtrack to the fork in the road where everything went wrong.

Note One: When you follow a fork and don't like the scenery, double back and take the other fork.

I didn't like the scenery in college. I liked what I saw as I gazed out the window of a truck, headed to where I was going to make someone happy by cheerfully hauling off their junk.

Jack Prescott was a buddy of mine from Montreal whom I had met at a French camp during the summer, so I made him my business partner. But Jack didn't have the heart of a founder.

Why is it that entrepreneurs so often decide they need a partner when they really just need a mentor?

Listen, when you feel like you're lost in the forest and you need help getting to the next level in business, don't go looking for a partner. Look for a mentor, a person who has successfully passed through the woods you feel lost in, a person who knows all the secret paths that lead out of that dark forest and into the sunshine.

Too often, a partner is just someone who will keep you company while you're both lost in the woods.

A true partner will have the heart of a founder, a heart that beats in rhythm with your own.

Pretty soon Jack and I were running three trucks, but something wasn't right, so I bought back Jack's half of the company that I had given him. The amount that I paid him was more than all the combined profits we had made together. The reason was simple. I believed in the company more deeply than he did, so I was willing to pay more money for his half of the company than he was willing to pay for mine.

Soon I had five trucks and eleven employees. We were doing half a million in revenue, and at twenty-four, I'd already bought my own house. From the outside, things seemed perfect. In reality, I was totally stressed out and hated coming in to work. The company I had seen in my mind when I got excited about junk hauling wasn't the company I was running.

When I thought about why work had stopped being fun, I realized it was pretty simple. I didn't like being around the people I'd hired, and at that point, they weren't keen on me either. The environment had turned toxic, and the team didn't believe in my vision or fit the culture I was trying to create.

The day I decided to fire all eleven employees was one of the scariest days of my life. It meant acknowledging that I'd failed as a leader, which I said when I let them all go. It also meant I'd be running the business solo for a few months while I rebuilt. But I knew in that moment that having the *right* people on board was more important than literally anything else. Since then, culture fit has been a nonnegotiable part of our hiring strategy.

Jason Smith was one of the new guys I hired, and he's still a friend today. He started out driving a truck for me, then came and worked in the office for a bit. Jason was the brains behind JunkNet, our booking and dispatch application. Jason gave us the gift of JunkNet (the first system of its kind, by the way!). What he found in return was that he had the entrepreneurial fire: a voice inside that told him to be his own founder.

With Jason's new understanding of failure—how to accept it, learn from it, and use that knowledge to succeed—he went on to start a tech company that he later sold for millions of dollars.

Dave Lodewyk was another breath of fresh air.

He started by driving a truck, made an hourly wage, rose through the ranks, and ran the office. But when he wanted to buy a 1-800-GOT-JUNK? franchise, we didn't quite have them ready to go. But Dave, like Jason, had learned to be a founder. So he went out and created a company that makes ski clothing that's sold all over North America today. Dave and Jason and I still hang out together.

Dave Lodewyk and Jason Smith were the beginning of what became our "culture of founders." You know you've created a culture of founders when everyone in your organization thinks and feels like an owner.

Things were definitely better, but I still knew something was missing.

I had followed a fork in the road called "partnership," but I didn't like the scenery, so this time, I doubled back and took the other fork marked "mentorship."

The mentors who came to my rescue were the members of YEO, the Young Entrepreneur's Organization. You had to be doing at least a million a year in sales to join. I can still remember telling them, "I'm not quite at the million." And they said, "Well, we like you, so you're close enough. And we believe you're gonna get there."

They welcomed me in and showed me how to get to the next level.

So now I was meeting people with $10 million or $20 million or $100 million businesses. And all I could think was, "Look at my crappy little junk-removal company doing not even a million dollars a year." I felt like I didn't have the money or the clarity of vision to get where I wanted to go. I'm not sure I even knew where I wanted to go.

So I went all alone to my parents' little cabin on the seashore to see if I could figure out what was wrong.

What I'm about to tell you is really important. In hindsight, it was probably the most impactful thing I ever did to shape my future.

After wandering around that cabin for a while in a funk, I sat down on the dock and thought, "Right now I'm trapped in this doom loop. But this isn't the way I do things. I'm an optimistic person."

So I pulled out a sheet of paper and said out loud, "Okay, what could pure possibility look like if nothing was in my way? What could this company look like in five years? Don't think about your lack of money, your lack of education, or the mistakes you've made. Just dream."

So I painted a word picture of the happiest future I could imagine, one page, double-sided.

It started with, "We will be in the top thirty metros in North America by the end of 2003."

I think I had the number thirty in my head because I knew there were thirty cities bigger than Vancouver in North America. If my junk-removal business worked in Vancouver, why shouldn't it work in every other city at least as big?

I kept on imagining things:

"We're going to be on The Oprah Winfrey show."

"We're gonna be the FedEx of junk removal."

"Clean, shiny trucks."

"On-time service."

"Up-front rates."

"Friendly, uniformed drivers."

And the drivers would always be smiling when they knocked on the customer's door! The people who opened those doors would be smiling, too!

And the drivers were going to be incredibly polite, helpful, and friendly.

And there were lots of other things on that list that made me proud and happy when I saw them in my mind.

Exactly what else was in my Painted Picture of "What I Want the Future to Look Like" doesn't really matter.

What matters is what's on *your* list.

What do you want your future to look like? Do you have the crazy courage to want that future, even though you have no idea how to make it happen? Are you willing to paint a word picture on a sheet of paper that includes all the details of the dream you'd like to see come true?

When I started reading what I had written, I went from an absolute doom-loop, pessimistic future to, "Oh my gosh, I can see this happening!"

My Painted Picture began with a thousand words that let me see in full color what I wanted. It wasn't, "I hope to do this," or, "I'm gonna try to do this."

I looked at that paper and said, "I'm gonna do this."

When you've seen in your mind what you want your future to look like, and you've painted a word picture on a sheet of paper, it somehow becomes more attainable.

Note Two: At the moment of commitment, the universe conspires to assist you.

The person who said that lived a couple of hundred years ago, and people have been quoting him ever since. But what interests me most is what he said next: "Whatever you can do, or dream you can do, begin it. Boldness has genius, power, and magic in it. Begin it now."

The secret to finding the dream that will burn so brightly in your heart that it pierces through the darkness and lights your way is this:

> **Note Three:** Don't worry about how you're going to make it happen.

There will be lots of time, later, to figure out how to do it. But first, you've got to light a fire in your heart. You've got to shut down your logical mind when it tries desperately to talk you out of your vision of the future. "Oh...well how the heck are you going to do that? You know that's not going to happen. You're not qualified to do that. You need to get your head out of the clouds. Who do you think you are? You're just setting yourself up for disappointment."

We all have that voice in our heads. Don't let it rob you of a bright future.

Another life-changing thing I did at that cabin was read Michael Gerber's book, *The E-Myth*, from cover to cover. It rocked me so hard that as soon as I finished it, I read it from cover to cover again.

I left that seaside cabin feeling on top of the world. I had discovered why I was unhappy, and I knew what I had to do to fix it.

I had learned from Michael's book that people don't fail; systems do. And I had learned that I needed to set my business up like a franchise, because franchises succeed due to systems.

What I needed was systems.

I developed those systems as I stumbled along—failure, success, failure, success, failure, success—until things began getting better, system by system.

Thank you, Michael.

CHAPTER 6

STARTING OVER AGAIN

Now I had a piece of paper in my pocket—the one I had written at that seaside cabin—that told me to look for people who take their happiness with them wherever they go. People who talk back and forth and enjoy each other's company as the day flies by. Because, you know, the job isn't really about hauling junk. It's about having fun together as we travel across town in a truck, making people happy.

Having just painted a clear picture of the people I needed, I was able to recognize—and recruit—that merry band of adventurers I had seen in my mind. These were definitely the right people.

And you know what? It turns out that the right people usually know a lot of other right people. They would often bring in their roommates and friends, and the vibe was entirely different. The vibe—and the people—were happy, hungry, hard-working, and hands-on.

What I had been searching for was the entrepreneurial spirit. I needed to be around people who saw possibilities and who had the courage, confidence, and craziness to go for it. I surrounded myself with those types of people: happy, hungry, hardworking, and hands-on—the 4Hs is what we call them.

Then I took five of my key people back to that same cottage on the seashore. One of those key people was Jesse Korzan. Jesse had the heart of a founder, and I'll never forget when, years later, Jesse and Nick Wood went out and got 1-800-GOT-JUNK? tattoos.

And they hadn't even been drinking.

Jesse and Nick decided to make my company their own.

Those are the kind of people it takes to succeed. Jesse and Nick are the kind of people you need.

I had been reading Jim Collins's book, *Good to Great*, where he says that every company has a set of values and it's incredibly important to communicate them.

I put Jim's big idea to the group. "Jim Collins says, 'Your values are who you are, not who you want to be.' You're either honest or not. You value friendships or you don't. It's not who we see ourselves being; it's who we really are as a company. So, what are our values?"

Then, I handed out stacks of Post-It notes and said, "Write down the words that describe who we already are. Just one word at a time, on a separate Post-It note." The windows overlooking the water became the sticky board for our Post-It notes. There were four hundred of them.

I said, "Now let's start grouping them together."

If there were two words that were similar, we put them together. Clusters of Post-It notes quickly began to form. In an hour, almost every one of those four hundred words fit into four categories, which we called:

- Passion
- Integrity
- Professionalism
- Empathy

Smiling, we said, "That's who we are." Everyone agreed. It was so crystal clear. "Our values are PIPE."

And I made myself a promise never to hire anyone who didn't have all four of those attributes.

I was looking for more Jesses and Nicks.

CHAPTER 7

DISCONNECT/ RECONNECT

And then there was Paul Guy.

I met Paul through Cameron Herold, who was in my Young Entrepreneur Organization forum. Cameron had been a senior guy at College Pro Painters, a company I really admired. Their franchisees paid college kids to paint houses. And if those franchisees ran their businesses as instructed, it became a win/win/win. The college student made enough money to pay for school, the homeowner got a beautiful paint job, and the franchisee made a nice living.

When I first started talking about franchising,

Cameron said, "Oh, you want an experienced franchise guy who knows how to make things happen? You need to meet Paul Guy. He's the one you need to help you develop your prototype."

I met Paul, hired him, and we worked together for a couple of years. Our original thought was to employ college students, like the College Pro Painters model. But Paul and I were out of step with each other. He would often challenge my decisions, and I would take it personally. We were butting heads constantly. And the student franchise thing wasn't really working for us. We began to think about changing to a full-time, professional franchise model. Unsure of what to do, I found it to be a stressful time.

Paul's office was right across the hall from mine, and the head-butting was getting worse. I forget what it was that pushed me over the edge, but one day I walked into Paul's office ready to lock horns with him like two rams on a mountaintop, each one trying to push the other off. I said, "You know, I don't think this is working out."

He said, "Really?"

"Yes, really."

"What do you want to do about it?"

I said, "I think we should end this."

"So you're telling me I'm fired?"

"Yeah, you're fired."

"When do you want me to leave?"

"How about right now?"

Paul said, "Okay."

And I left the office for the rest of that day.

But Paul kept coming to work like nothing had happened! It was weird, so I was avoiding him. He didn't really want to leave the company, and he couldn't simply abandon the student franchisees he was helping, so Paul just kept coming in every day. At the end of the third day, I went into his office and said, "Paul, I know you've been traveling back to Toronto to visit your girlfriend, Nicole (who's now his wife). Have you ever thought of moving back there and running the first full-time, professional, 1-800-GOT-JUNK? franchise?"

He looked at me and smiled.

And I smiled.

And we had this moment of possibility.

I never once doubted that Paul had passion, integrity, professionalism, and empathy. What drove me crazy was that his style of communication was very different from my own. During that glowing moment of possibility, I remember thinking, "I fired this guy three days ago and he refused to leave." It made me admire him a little.

Paul interrupted my thoughts. "Okay, let's do this."

We connected on the idea of Paul running the first 1-800-GOT-JUNK? franchise. We talked about it continuously for the next few days. Two years of frustration and anxiety completely vanished, and we became the closest of friends.

Have you ever become friends with a rival? I'll bet you have.

You've played with a pair of magnets, right? Position them one way and they repel each other. But if you align them differently, *click!*—they become inseparable.

The opposite of strong emotions is indifference.

Paul and I were never indifferent to one another. We were connected by strong emotion. At first that emotion was negative, but it quickly became positive, almost as if someone had flipped a switch.

A switch labeled "POSSIBILITY."

I share this with you because there's a solid chance that your most annoying rival is just a possibility away from becoming the strongest and most committed of your allies. You just need to turn strong emotions into a shared vision of a possible future.

> **Note Four:** Possibilities are the beginning of every adventure.

When Paul became the first serious, professional full-time 1-800-GOT-JUNK? franchise owner, he ordered a new dump truck built exactly like the trucks I used, complete with 1-800-GOT-JUNK? signage. Then he threw all his belongings in the back of that open-box truck and aimed it at Toronto.

His life's belongings. Literally everything he owned.

And then the morning dawned for Paul to begin his epic adventure driving that dump truck from Vancouver to Toronto, the Canadian version of Los Angeles to New York. It was the magical beginning of something new. If this was a movie, right now is when the theme music would begin to play.

That theme music ended when Paul called me from Abbotsford, about a hundred and sixty kilometers east of Vancouver. "I'm losing all my marketing material out the back of the truck." The tarp wasn't secured properly and had blown away.

Why am I telling you this?

I'm telling you these embarrassing, true stories

because sooner or later you're going to do something so incredibly Homer Simpson that you hit your forehead with the heel of your hand and say, "D'oh!" When that happens, don't fall apart and think less of yourself. Moments like this are part of every adventure.

> **Note Five:** When you're having an adventure, you wish you were safe at home. But when you're safe at home, you wish you were having an adventure.

If you ever say to yourself, "Maybe this wasn't such a good idea..." that's the one, sure sign your adventure has begun!

The misadventure with the tarp wasn't even our biggest mistake.

It was May 29, 1999. The phone rang. I answered it. Paul said, "I've driven a dump truck from coast to coast and put all my money—and all my brother's money—into a junk-hauling business in Toronto. And I just learned that the City of Toronto will haul away *anything* for free!"

Hand to the forehead. "D'oh."

I'm glad Paul couldn't see my face, because I was terrified. But that's not what Paul needed from me. He needed me to have his back. He needed me to talk him through this. He needed encouragement. So I said, "Paul, everything's going to be okay. I'm sure there's a way to make this work. Get out there and start marketing. Trust that this is going to happen. Have some faith. We're going to build this together."

When a person needs riches and you give them riches, you enrich them.

When a person needs courage and you give them courage, you encourage them.

It turned out that people didn't know who to call to have the City of Toronto haul stuff away. And the city had a lot of requirements and restrictions. For example, they wouldn't go into your house, your basement, your garage, or even walk across your yard to get your stuff. You had to stack everything neatly on the curb and make brownies for the removal team.

I made up the part about the brownies.

Did I mention that Paul is now collecting thousands of loads a month in Toronto? That's right, *a month.* And all it took was clean, shiny trucks; friendly, uniformed employees; and a sincere offer of effortless, full-service junk removal. "We'll climb into your attic, crawl into your basement, dig through your shed, whatever you need. All you have to do is point."

But there was a moment during Paul's adventure when he felt like he had made the biggest mistake of his life. "Why-oh-why didn't I pick up the telephone when I was in Vancouver and find out that the City of Toronto would haul away people's junk for free? It would have been such an easy phone call to make."

Thank goodness Paul didn't make that phone call. It would have blown out his candle, squashed his hope, and cost him thousands of truckloads every month.

Paul Guy proved that full-service junk removal wasn't just a Vancouver-only thing. And he also proved that long-term, fully committed, full-time Franchise Partners would be the secret to our success.

College students were not our answer.

Now all we needed was a chief operating officer who knew how to crank the handle and fire this thing up.

CHAPTER 8

WHEN NITRO MEETS GLYCERIN

Cameron Herold became an important mentor to me after I was accepted into the Young Entrepreneurs Organization. But I distinctly remember him chuckling at a scatterbrained comment I made one day, then saying, "Brian, I would never work for you."

Paul and I were now doing a little less than $2 million a year between Toronto and Vancouver. So I called Cameron and said, "You did a good thing when you connected me with Paul Guy. So now I need you to come in and help me scale up our franchise systems. You did it with Boyd Autobody, and you helped turn College Pro Painters into a miracle company. Cameron, I need your help." My goal was to have 250 Franchise Partners with system-wide sales of $100 million by the end of 2006.

He said, "Okay, I'll come and consult for seventy-five dollars an hour, but this is just temporary."

Three weeks into the process, we were having so much fun and making so much progress that he said, "Do you remember the day I told you I'd never work for you?"

"Yeah. I definitely remember."

"Well, I've changed my mind."

I had been the best man in Cameron's wedding, and now he was our COO. But I hadn't forgotten the lessons I'd learned from my first partnership, so I kept Cameron's involvement at arm's reach.

This wasn't easy, because Cameron and I were joined at the hip. He was as emotionally involved with my company as I was. We bled blue and green. We never took off our 1-800-GOT-JUNK? vests.

We were dangerous together.

Really dangerous.

We talked in Chapter 5 about the importance of having a Painted Picture of the future, so I thought I'd give you an example of what one of those looks and sounds like.

You'll notice that a Painted Picture speaks of what we believe will happen in the future as though it has already happened. In other words, we use present-tense verbs to describe the future. For example, we could say, "1-800-GOT-JUNK? is North America's household name in junk removal," when in reality, we were only in Vancouver and Toronto and a couple of other towns.

Using present-tense verbs lets you tell your brain exactly what the future is going to look like, so your brain can more quickly alert you when your actions are taking you off-target.

We paint a new picture every four years.

This was a particularly important one.

I'm sharing this Painted Picture in its original language, word for word.

THE VISION

The 1-800-GOT-JUNK? vision is one of growth through leadership. Our short-term goal, decided upon in 1998, is to be present in North America's thirty largest metros by the end of 2003.

Our following vision, or what we call our "Painted Picture," is a descriptive image of what 1-800-GOT JUNK? will look like at the end of 2003:

1-800-GOT-JUNK? is North America's household name in junk removal. When the city garbage collectors won't take it, 1-800-GOT-JUNK? will.

PRESENCE

1-800-GOT-JUNK? has a presence in North America's top thirty metropolitan areas with 118 Franchise Partners in total.

MONITORING GROWTH

Our tracking systems tell us clients are impressed with our commitment to provide them with on-time service and up-front rates. Clients find order in all dealings with 1-800-GOT-JUNK? from the booking of the appointment, to the call ahead, to the presentation of the price list and the thorough cleanup. With more than half of our business coming from repeat clients and word of mouth, the world recognizes 1-800-GOT-JUNK? as the leader in junk removal.

The pulse of our business can be read as easily as a stopwatch. Reporting is simple to read and easy to digest. Franchise Partners are given an accurate indication of what's working, what's not, where we're profitable, where we're not, and where and when innovation is due.

IMAGE

Our image is cohesive. Everyone who comes in contact with 1-800-GOT-JUNK?, including clients, team members, media, and investors, all notice our squeaky-clean trucks, our clean and professional uniforms, and all components of the catchy and memorable 1-800-GOT-JUNK? brand.

MEDIA

The media has helped us grow at an annual growth rate of 90 percent. The 1-800-GOT-JUNK? story has been carried throughout North America through newswire services, such as Reuters and the Associated Press.

SYSTEMS

Proper systems have been recognized as a key component to corporate growth and the evolution of our program. Working toward complete systemization of all components of the business has proven to promote both efficiency and profitability.

Our hiring systems attract the best workers for the positions we offer. Our systems and image have given rise to our success at attracting team members who are proud to be part of our vision and mission.

TRAINING AND COACHING

1-800-GOT-JUNK? teaches, encourages, and rewards innovation. Corporate team members and Franchise Partners are trained thoroughly and consistently by following our comprehensive operations manuals and training systems. The team members of the

Franchise Partners are also trained with the same attention to detail.

SUPPORT CENTER

The Client Services Center is an exciting, fast-paced environment filled with our energetic frontline team members. Each Franchise Partner is assigned a support rep who oversees the management of the Franchise Partner's territory. Calls, faxes, and web-based orders are filtered through the Center and directed to a team of dedicated agents serving a particular group of territories. This gives clients the personal service typically found in a smaller office.

MENTOR BOARD OF ADVISORS

We have an MBA (Mentor Board of Advisors) that has helped us chart and maintain our course. We have a team of people who each have a mentor—someone they can turn to for advice.

BEYOND 2003

As we approach the end of 2003, here are our medium-term goals: to have 250 Franchise Partners with system-wide sales of $100 million by the end of 2006.

AND...IT WORKED!

Cameron Herold helped me paint that picture, and then he helped me make it a reality. Did you notice our medium-term goal of $100 million by the end of 2006? We finished even higher.

Taking us from system-wide sales of less than $2 million to just over $100 million in just seven years, Cameron Herold was exactly the right COO, at exactly the right time.

CHAPTER 9

ENTHUSIASM IS CONTAGIOUS

Tom Rypma was twenty-nine when I met him. 1-800-GOT-JUNK? had been featured on the front cover of *Profit* magazine, which is sort of the Canadian version of *Fortune*. Tom had just read the article when he called and said, "I'm going to be in Vancouver, and I want to meet with you."

We really hit it off. I knew this was a great guy. He wanted to run the Calgary franchise, which is where he was from. We were getting close to doing a deal when Tom called me and said, "A buddy of mine was just in a bad kayaking accident. He's in the hospital, so I need to delay."

Tom needed to do what true friendship requires. Later, he moved to San Francisco where he became hugely successful working for a company that sells medical equipment. But Tom never quit watching us from a distance. He followed our success and was happy for us. Then one day he called again and said, "Listen, I'm the top performer for this big company in San Francisco, but I'm not loving it. What do you think about me bringing 1-800-GOT-JUNK? to San Francisco?"

Tom did take 1-800-GOT-JUNK? to San Francisco, and his success there has been spectacular. I secretly suspect the city would elect Tom as mayor if he ever chose to run for office.

But why would he do that when he's having so much fun?

Jason Smith and Dave Lodewyk. Paul Guy and Cameron Herold. Tom Rypma. These were the kinds of people who became the heart and soul of the new 1-800-GOT-JUNK?.

Happy, hungry, hardworking, and hands-on. People with the heart of a founder.

Sometimes, you can have the heart of a founder and not actually own a business.

Getting on the front page of the *Vancouver Province* newspaper gave us the courage to call the Canadian equivalent of *60 Minutes*, a show called *The Journal*. So we called them up and said, "I've got an awesome story for you!"

They sent out reporters and camera people, and we were on national TV during prime time. "Tight Summer Job Market in Vancouver and da-da-da."

> **Note Six:** Never email your story pitch. You've got to pick up the phone and call.

By 2002, we had a PR department. It was just one person.

His name was Tyler Wright, and he had no experience whatsoever.

> **Note Seven:** A person isn't measured by their current set of skills, but by how effectively they use what they've got.

Tyler Wright was a super tall, slender young guy with boundless energy. You couldn't help but feel his presence when he was in the room. So I taught him my secret of how to get press and entrusted him with one of my goals: *The Oprah Winfrey Show.*

Oprah was part of the Painted Picture I had created that day at the cabin by the seashore. So, I put a huge decal on the wall that said, "Can you imagine?" Everyone who walked past that wall for the next few days asked, "What does that mean? What does that mean?"

Then, when no one was looking, I put another decal on the wall: "Can you imagine being featured on *The Oprah Winfrey Show*?" And then I left a pile of markers on a little table beneath the decal.

Pretty soon, Laurie Baggio took a marker and wrote, "Can you imagine 1-800-GOT-JUNK? in Australia?" Four years later, we were there.

Little kids are taught not to mark on the walls. But when you want big kids to share a shining vision of a possible future, a wall and some markers might be exactly what you need.

People came up with big, bold ideas, and they'd sign their names below each one. This is how they made the company their own and became founders like Jesse and Nick who got the 1-800-GOT-JUNK? tattoos.

I'd see Tyler standing in front of that wall every day, reading the decal I had placed there that said, "Can you imagine being featured on *The Oprah Winfrey Show*?" He would slowly nod his head up and down so that you could almost hear his mind whispering, "We're gonna make that happen."

And then he'd walk away from that wall, stand up at his desk, put on his phone headset, and over the top of that headset, he'd put a curly blue wig. I need you to imagine a tall, slender guy with size-sixteen-and-a-half shoes wearing a curly blue wig. And we're not talking ocean blue. We're talking glow-in-the-dark, radioactive blue.

Tyler always stood up when he was pitching a story, and he'd put on that blue wig to get himself in a crazy spirit. Then he'd pitch and pitch and pitch every sort of medium in cities and towns all across the United States and Canada. Tyler Wright got us lots and lots of stories.

One day Tyler began running through the building screaming hysterically, "I did it! I did it!" Everyone looked a bit panicked, like they were thinking, "What's going on here? Is Tyler losing his mind?" When he noticed that everyone in the building was staring at him in confusion, he shouted, "Oprah! Oprah! I got Oprah!"

Again, we were all thinking the same thought, "Did that really happen?" Tyler was vibrating and shaking as he whispered, "They need us to be in Los Angeles tomorrow morning at 6:00 a.m."

That's when we believed him, and that's when the party began. I'll bet you could put your ear to the wall in that building today and still hear the echo of our celebration.

> **Note Eight:** Specifics are always more believable than generalities.

His statement, "I got Oprah!" left us wondering. But when he said, "They need us to be in Los

Angeles tomorrow morning at 6:00 a.m.," we were convinced.

Then someone said, "Wait. Did you just say we have to be in Los Angeles tomorrow morning at 6:00 a.m.?"

Tears in his eyes, Tyler was leaning forward with his hands on his knees, gasping for air. All he could do was nod his head yes.

Now we were all looking at each other, collectively thinking the same thought for the third time: "We don't have any trucks in Los Angeles. And Vancouver to LA is over 2,000 kilometers."

Tyler motioned for us to gather around him. After he caught his breath, he said, "Okay, so they want us to come down to LA to film this woman who wants to help her mother who's a hoarder. She's got this small, one-bedroom apartment. She can't even sleep in her bed 'cause there's junk on both sides and it's just crazy."

The realistic part of my brain was whispering, "If we left this very moment, we couldn't be in Los

Angeles with trucks by 6:00 a.m. tomorrow," but my blue-wig brain was saying, "Tyler got us on Oprah, so we're gonna make this happen!" And then my blue-wig brain said, "Get on the phone with Tom Rypma in San Francisco and ask him to start driving some trucks toward Los Angeles."

Always listen to your blue-wig brain.

We hopped on a plane, flew to LA, met Tom Rypma and the producers at 6:00 a.m., and started cleaning out this woman's home.

And then I got invited to Chicago to be on stage with Oprah and talk about the hoarder video she was about to show. When she said, "Brian Scudamore," my long-awaited four and a half minutes had begun.

After Tyler Wright accomplished the impossible, everyone in our company began to stare at our "Can You Imagine?" wall with a new kind of intensity.

CHAPTER 10

THE BLUE WIG IS WHERE YOU FIND IT

If this chapter offers a lesson to be learned, it's this:

> **Note Nine:** The right thing to do doesn't always make sense at first.

All this free press attracted a lot of Franchise Partners. So one of our go-getter partners, Nick Wood, put together a group of six of them as a sort of Franchise Advisory Council to give us feedback about what's working and what's not. Pretty soon they were up in arms saying, "Our businesses aren't growing quickly enough. We need more professional marketing—advertising—instead of just guerrilla marketing, which relies on free stories in the press. We need to professionalize."

Lots of complaints. Lots of complaints.

I said to the team, "We gotta do something about this." So I asked the Advisory Council, "Where's the toughest city to get awareness? Where is it impossible to stand out?"

They said, "Las Vegas. You can't stand out in Vegas."

So I said, "We're gonna have a meeting in Las Vegas about how to take our branding to the next level. We're gonna have some fun, and we're gonna stand out. If we can make it there, we can make it anywhere."

Seriously, I almost started singing that old Frank Sinatra song, "I want to wake up in that city that doesn't sleep and find I'm king of the hill, top of the heap."

So Tyler and I and a few others came up with an idea that was too crazy for one person to have come up with on their own.

Ten of us spent three dollars apiece on a curly blue wig and twenty-six dollars on a bowling shirt branded with 1-800-GOT-JUNK?, then boarded an airplane for Las Vegas. Total investment: $290, plus plane tickets.

We went everywhere in Vegas as a group.

> **Note Ten:** One person wearing a bowling shirt and a curly blue wig is a nut. Ten people in bowling shirts and curly blue wigs are magic.

"Are you guys a band?"

"Are you a bachelor party?"

"Who are you?"

"What's going on? What am I missing out on?"

We wandered into the Hard Rock Hotel because the whole building was glowing with blue neon.

And everyone in there was wearing Armani and looking cool.

We were the dorks who looked like twenty-nine bucks.

Within minutes, we were mobbed by curious people who wanted to know what was going on. And the bigger the crowd got, the farther away people came from to be part of it.

> **Note Eleven:** Nothing draws a crowd like a crowd.

We had these temporary 1-800-GOT-JUNK? tattoos and little spray bottles, so we began branding the backs of people's hands with 1-800-GOT-JUNK?.

You weren't cool unless you had one.

Ten happy, friendly people connected by the shared vision of a possible future—that's all we were. But everyone looked at us like we were rock stars. Bottom line: we stood out in Vegas and became the talk of the town as thousands of people showed their 1-800-GOT-JUNK? tattoos to thousands of other people who wished they had one, too.

We showed all our Franchise Partners, and ourselves, that guerrilla marketing could work anywhere.

Back home, our local hockey team, the Vancouver Canucks, were in the playoffs, and they hadn't been in a long time. So Tyler called the press and said we were going to be handing out blue wigs to everyone who attended a Canucks game because we wanted the Canucks to know we were excited and behind them.

We wanted to fill that stadium with blue-wig spirit. So Tyler began making phone calls all over North America, buying up every blue wig he could find. We arrived at the hockey game with more than two thousand blue wigs loaded into a 1-800-GOT-JUNK? truck that we drove right on to the Vancouver Canucks' private property. We weren't supposed to be there, but we were handing out free wigs to a lot of excited people, so what were they going to say?

> **Note Twelve:** It's easier to get forgiveness than permission.

We put those wigs on people's heads like we were crowning the Queen of England. And people wore them that way, too. It was the tattoos in Las Vegas all over again. Everyone who got a blue wig was proud of it, and everyone who didn't get one wanted one.

When you're looking at tens of thousands of people in a packed stadium and one person in thirty is wearing a neon-blue wig, it really lights the place up.

We were on the front page of the newspaper again with our truck and its huge 1-800-GOT-JUNK? logo/phone number on the side of it. But the even bigger story is what happened in the parking lot right before the game.

The top three news stations showed up at six o'clock so that Cameron, our COO, and Tyler, our PR guy, could explain to everyone watching live television why we were giving out blue wigs.

Every TV station, radio station, newspaper, and

magazine wanted to be part of that excitement. Tyler and Cameron were interviewed by sixty different media outlets before it was all over.

Later, Tyler Wright decided to pitch us to CNBC. Mike Hegedus was CNBC's "Why didn't I think of that?" business guy, and everyone liked him. So Mike came out and filmed us for a feature story on 1-800-GOT-JUNK?.

But then Tyler took the whole thing to another level. When our feature had been edited and was scheduled to air, Tyler sent a big box to Mike Hegedus at CNBC in New Jersey. In it were two blue wigs and two 1-800-GOT-JUNK? jackets. Tyler wasn't sure what would happen, but he just felt like he should send those.

So, live on *Squawk Box*, just after they showed our clip, Mike Hegedus gets up and says to the host of the show, "Check out how awesome these guys are! I got this big box addressed to me, so I opened it up. Look! Two blue wigs and two jackets!" Then he puts on the jacket and gives the other one to the host to put on. Then they put the blue wigs on just as it was fading to commercial.

Note Thirteen: Enthusiasm is contagious.

WHY AM I DOING THIS?

By this time, it was 2007, and I couldn't believe how far we'd come. I never imagined I'd have this kind of company with this many passionate people around me. Then I got a huge surprise: the biggest garbage-collection company in the world wanted in.

The folks at Waste Management invited me to a super swanky resort—a real-life private island with all the ultra-lux bells and whistles. It felt like *Lifestyles of the Rich and Famous.*

There we were—three of us on a boat, waiting for

the salmon to bite—when one of the big dogs said, "We want to buy your company."

"It's not for sale."

"We're talking somewhere between 75 and 100 million dollars."

This was the moment of truth. It's easy to talk about what you would or wouldn't do, but it's not until you're actually in the moment that you know for certain. As I always have, I listened to my gut. And it was telling me not to sell.

"I'm flattered by your interest, and I'm honored that you think so highly of my company, but I've only just gotten started."

They looked at each other in confusion, so I continued. "1-800-GOT-JUNK? is attracting a lot of great people who are learning what it means to be an owner, an entrepreneur, an employer of others. And we're gaining momentum as a big, united, blue-wig team that is spreading all across the United States, Canada, and Australia. For me, there's no happiness like the joy of seeing someone seize an opportunity and run with it. I'm sorry, guys, but I really want to keep what I've got."

For the record, being on a little boat kilometers from shore with two garbage company executives you've just said no to? Insanely scary!

CHAPTER 12

UNTHINKABLE

Tyler Wright was an avid hiker. I think it was his way of powering down.

So no one gave it a second thought when Tyler said he was going on a really long hike between Vancouver and Whistler. But when he wasn't back at the end of a week, a lot of people started to get concerned. A bunch of us rallied around the question, "What would Tyler do to find Tyler?" And we immediately knew that Tyler would leverage the press to gather a record number of rescue experts and experienced searchers with helicopters using GoPro cameras to scour every inch of that dense, eighty-square-kilometer forest.

The search for Tyler Wright became the largest search-and-rescue effort in the history of British Columbia. But the only thing anyone ever found was a single footprint from a size-sixteen-and-a-half hiking boot that was probably made on the second day of his hike.

For Tyler to be gone was unthinkable. I've never been able to make peace with it. There's something inside me that still expects him to call and say, "Hey! Where did you move the office? I finished my hike, but when I got back to work, all of you were gone."

Today, when the 1-800-GOT-JUNK? partners gather from around the world each year for the 1-800-GOT-JUNK? conference, we give an award to the person who most perfectly captured Tyler's blue-wig spirit that year. It's a tremendous honor to receive the Wright Way Award. Everyone gets a little choked up.

And then a second unthinkable thing happened. It wasn't nearly as tragic as Tyler's disappearance, but it was painful nonetheless.

Do you remember when I said Cameron and I

were dangerous together? Well, we were both about to learn that it was time for him to leave.

When the practices, systems, and procedures had finally been perfected, Cameron and I began to make some incredibly impulsive decisions together. With revenues over $100 million a year, what we needed most was back-office discipline, but neither of us was very good at that. We didn't have the patience to sit on a good idea. We never said, "Okay, let's talk about that for a while." Instead, we went all in.

I'd say, "Hey, Cameron, what do you think of this?" And *boom!*—off he'd go to get it done.

When you add one spontaneous person to another spontaneous person, you don't get double the spontaneity—it goes exponential. Like a nuclear reactor with insufficient coolant.

We spent a lot of money. Fire. Ready. Aim.

One of our ideas was to prove that truck marketing—we call it parketing—would produce significant increases in business. It was easy to lease parking spaces at high-visibility shopping centers, so our idea was to park a 1-800-GOT-JUNK? truck right at the edge of every busy intersection where they would basically be giant billboards. And the name of our company is our phone number! And it tells them what we do! We'll be everywhere! Woo-hoo!

Our goal was to get Franchise Partners to buy more trucks, so Cameron said, "You know what? We have four trucks in Vancouver right now. We're quadrupling our fleet. We're going to have sixteen trucks!"

It was a great idea in theory, but it was too much money, too big of an idea. And there was no one there to talk us down from it.

We did a lot of things like that.

Like the time we went out and started eight corporate locations and hired eight new managers to run them. Every single one of those new locations failed because we had become hands-off; the managers weren't as invested in our success. It was a tough lesson on the importance of being hands-on in your business.

In a humbling moment, Cameron and I looked at each other and said, "Okay, maybe we're not so good at this."

Things were beginning to crumble and fail. We were starting to see the foundation crack.

Even though revenue had skyrocketed by the end of 2006, there were still lots of challenges ahead. And we knew that the way we were running things wasn't sustainable.

Cameron and I had grown the business beyond the length of our shadows. It was bigger than both of us. This was a dangerous time. Cameron and I were a great team, but not for a company of the size that 1-800-GOT-JUNK? had become.

We were the best of friends. But what we were doing had to end.

CHAPTER 13

STARTING ALL OVER AGAIN. AGAIN.

I needed a new COO. I wish I could tell you that I chose this person wisely and that we lived happily ever after, but I promised to tell this story honestly, so no, none of that happened.

It was like "Goldilocks and the Three Bears": "This porridge is too hot... This porridge is too cold... This porridge is just right."

Well, I went from too-hot porridge to too-cold porridge. I hired a key executive from Starbucks—the president of one of their divisions, in fact.

On paper, this person was exactly who we needed. In reality, I'd overcorrected the problem.

> **Note Fourteen:** When you're out of balance in one direction, be careful not to overcompensate, or else you might find yourself equally out of balance in the other direction.

During the next fourteen months, our business dropped by a third.

I honestly thought I was going to lose the whole thing.

The problem was that our new COO didn't have the blue-wig spirit. I watched helplessly as the life-force drained slowly out of my company, and the soul of 1-800-GOT-JUNK? began to fade.

Finally, I stepped in and said, "Enough." It was a low moment.

I ran the business by myself for the next two years, even though my Franchise Partners were telling me I wasn't the right guy to do it. But I already knew that. I also knew it was better to have no help than the wrong help. And I was looking, looking, looking for the right person.

Eventually, I drew a line down the middle of a sheet of paper. On the left side, I wrote all the things a business needs that I'm good at and I love to do. On the right side, I wrote all the things a business needs that I'm bad at and I hate to do.

On the "hate to do" side of the paper were things like:

- Reviewing financials
- Creating business plans
- Budgeting
- Hiring
- Building teams

But this disciplined, organized business person I was searching for still needed to be sales-driven and able to execute a plan based on vision and adventure. They had to have the heart of an enthusiastic founder, not the heart of a clerk.

When I finally had a clear vision of exactly who I

needed, I wrote down their characteristics in as much detail as I could imagine.

"I am a high-energy, results-driven leader. People on my team know we play to win. When the goal is clear, we don't let anything get in our way. I work hard to ensure my team is composed of top talent and that their teams each have the right people, in the right seats. I develop my people to be their best and to work hard to grow our business—to believe in and realize the possibilities we set. I thrive on having full responsibility for revenue and sales growth.

"I am passionate about building strategic plans that translate into results—plans that allow me to lead the charge with focused execution, tight accountability, and frequent celebration.

"I am looking to partner with an entrepreneur whose vision is crystal clear—someone who thrives on figuring out how to turn impossible ideas into reality. I love Canada and have always wanted to call Vancouver home."

Then, I showed those paragraphs to different people outside my company.

Two of those people looked at my list and said the same thing, "Wow. There's only one person in the whole world who fits that description." And then they both gave me the same name.

When I showed the list to Cameron Herold, he said the same thing, too: "Wow. There's only one person in the whole world who fits that description. He and I started a fraternity together in college. He was member number one and I was member number two. After graduation, he went on to do some amazing things at a couple of companies. His name is Erik Church."

Erik Church was the same name the first two people had given me.

I'll bet you didn't see that coming. Neither did I.

Seriously, who would have ever dreamed that the person I desperately needed to replace Cameron Herold would be the cofounder of a college fraternity that he and Cameron had started together?

I contacted Erik, and we clicked immediately. It was obvious why he and Cameron had been friends. Miraculously, Erik agreed to accept the position of COO at 1-800-GOT-JUNK?.

This time, the porridge was just right.

> **Note Fifteen:** Don't hesitate to ask the universe for what you need.

One of the first things Erik and I agreed on was that the time had come to hire a director of sales and marketing with blue-wig spirit.

The man we needed was working for Paul Guy in Toronto. And because Paul is a true partner, he was willing to give him to us.

David St. James (DSJ) grew up selling stereos in his family's business. He was so incredibly good at it that Bose Stereo hired him to work in their corporate office.

Paul and David had known each other since high school, so when Paul's franchise got so big that he needed a full-time sales trainer and director of marketing, he reached out to DSJ.

When DSJ plugs into something, he gives it everything he's got. Shortly after he came to work for us, he asked our permission to wrap his car in the 1-800-GOT-JUNK? logo so it would be a sort of moving billboard people would see all over town. It worked so well that we later began incentivizing some of our employees with $3,000 if they were willing to wrap their vehicles, too.

But DSJ had wrapped his vehicle when the only incentive was to help us grow the company. DSJ had the heart of a founder.

He had done wonderful things for Paul. Now we needed him to send his high-voltage energy into the rest of our Franchise Partners.

DSJ and Erik and I agreed that the time had come to create those TV and radio ads our partners had long been asking for.

CHAPTER 14

DO YOU BELIEVE IN MAGIC?

Everyone has their own opinions about what makes an ad successful, but few people are able to write consistently successful ads.

We had heard about a remarkable, but reclusive, ad writer who doesn't accept phone calls from people who want to hire him. This sounded ridiculous to us, so I decided to call and see for myself.

His gatekeeper politely told me that I would have to pay $7,500 in advance and fly to Austin if I wanted to spend a day with the Wizard of Ads, and no, he would not talk to us on the telephone or answer our emails before we got there. She also told us that it was highly unlikely he would agree to write our ads for us, but that my team and I would leave Austin with valuable insight and advice about what to do, and what not to do. She said the most we could hope for was that the Wizard might recommend us to one of his forty-six partners around the world.

David, Erik, and I paid the money and flew to Texas.

It would have been worth the money just to see his campus. Twelve buildings sprawled across twenty-one acres, including a fabulous wizard's tower that overlooks the city of Austin from the top of a plateau that rises nine hundred feet above the city. And on the sidewalk leading to that tower, you discover a beautiful little chapel hanging off the edge of a cliff.

He held our meeting in a storeroom full of paintings.

It was a strange and wonderful day.

I have to admit I was a little bit worried when he began to give us his advice, because I felt he hadn't listened to our story long enough to develop a fully informed opinion of us. How could he possibly know what to do if he didn't really know who we are?

Just as I was thinking that thought, he showed us the diagram of a baseball diamond. "David Freeman is a famous screenwriting coach," he said, "who developed a technique for creating magnetically engaging characters in novels, movies, and TV shows. What I'm about to show you is a modification of David Freeman's technique. He calls it a character diamond."

Erik, DSJ, and I exchanged nervous glances. Why did we need to know about screenwriting? But we kept listening.

"For an imaginary character to be interesting, he or she has to be driven by two pairs of opposites. These four conflicting motivations will determine how that character thinks, speaks, acts, and sees the world."

Pointing at second base and home plate, he said, "People are attracted to a character because of the vertical opposites." Then, pointing at third base and first base, he said, "But they'll bond with that character because of the horizontal opposites."

That's when—without preface or explanation—he showed me screenshots of the leading characters in my three favorite movies when I was a kid: Willy Wonka, Doctor Dolittle, and Peter Pan. I was almost speechless. But when he showed me the leprechaun from Lucky Charms, I blurted out, "Have you been talking to my mother?"

"No."

"Then how did you know my favorite movies and breakfast cereal growing up?"

"Brian, you've been energized by happy, magical characters your entire life. It's one of the things that attracts people to you." Then he pointed to second base and said, "'Happy magic' is what goes right there."

"I don't understand."

"A brand with personality is an imaginary character in the mind of the public, just like characters in movies, TV shows, and novels. But for your advertising to ring true, your brand personality has to be built on something you're going to deliver without even having to think about it. Happy magic is what 1-800-GOT-JUNK? has always been about."

Then, with his finger still on second base, he spoke the phrase that has since become famous across the United States, Canada, and Australia: "We make junk disappear. All you have to do is point."

"You never told me how you knew about the movies and the cereal."

"Brian," he said, "your deepest desire is to deliver an upbeat, happy, magical experience. It shines out of every pore in your skin. I've never met anyone with a light inside them that burns as brightly as yours. I hope you're not offended."

"Offended? I'm delighted!"

"Tell me about your mother," he said. "I'm betting she gave you that crazy optimism. Am I right?"

He was right.

And after I told him about my mom, he agreed to write our ads for us.

CHAPTER 15

REAL MAGIC, SEEN FIRSTHAND

Victoria Lorber married her high school sweetheart. She was a better wife than he was a husband, so he and I never had a relationship. I wasn't exaggerating when I said, "I got a dad when I was seven."

Mom never made me feel like I was a mistake, or a burden, or even an inconvenience. She's always been my biggest cheerleader. Even when I was little, she would listen to my ideas and make me feel good about them. Not once in my life has she ever shaken her head and said, "Bad idea, Brian."

Mom's parents helped raise me while she got a

degree in ultrasound at the University of California, San Francisco. Grandpa and Grandma Lorber were down-to-earth, hardworking people who sold surplus merchandise in a questionable neighborhood, but they had the magical ability to make every life they touched a little better.

Just like Willy Wonka, Doctor Dolittle, and Peter Pan.

Sweep, clean, lift and carry, stack boxes, greet customers. I loved hanging out at their store. It was wonderful.

They gave me my first taste of entrepreneurship, and I thrived in that environment.

Working for my grandparents, I felt valuable. I felt included. They made me feel, perhaps for the first time, that I was exactly where I belonged.

Lorber's Surplus was an army surplus store in the Mission District in San Francisco, which at that time was a dodgy neighborhood. Businesses there got robbed all the time. The locksmith next door got hit repeatedly. So did the electrical shop on the other side of us. Everyone got robbed except Lorber's Surplus, even though our stuff—leather jackets, watches, things like that—would definitely have been the easiest to sell.

When I got older, I realized why my grandparents never got robbed.

The people who lived on the street in the Mission District knew my grandparents and liked them. Grandma Florence and Grandpa Kenny took the time to learn everyone's names and listen to their stories, and then they would call those people by name and wave at them when they saw them outside, and stop to ask them how they were doing. Grandma and Grandpa Lorber made street people feel welcome when they came into our store, even though they never gave them money when they asked for it.

Instead, my grandparents gave them dignity and hope. They would say, "You have a lot to offer the world. And I believe you have a bright future ahead of you. Please understand that we like you and we care about you very much, even though we're not going to do the thing you're asking us to do."

Looking back, it's pretty obvious the word among the street people was, "Don't let anyone mess with the Lorbers. They're our friends."

Mom is exactly like her parents. I was barely out of diapers when she gave me everything I needed to become a successful entrepreneur.

We played Candyland together until I invented my own Batman-versus-Superman board game, using a tiny little Batman and a tiny little Superman. It was like Candyland in that you would roll the dice and go around the board and branch off on different paths, but my game was more of an action/adventure.

I charged her fifty cents every time she wanted to play it with me.

She acted like fifty cents was a bargain price. And she acted like it was the most wonderful game she had ever played.

I learned from my mom that it was okay to make money by making people smile. It's no coincidence that I'm still doing this today.

One summer when I was a few years older, the kid across the street started washing cars for three dollars each. A sheet of plywood and a can of paint later, I had a sign directly across from his—but my sign said, "CAR WASH $2." Then I convinced some friends in my school to hold signs at the corner of the busier street a block away.

Our revenues exploded! Well, as much as they could at $2 a pop. We couldn't believe how much money we were making. Our street became famous as the car-washing street. My neighbor and I both made a lot more money by competing with each other than either of us would have made alone.

When Mom heard about it, she said she was extremely proud of me.

My mother encouraged me constantly.

Is there anyone in your life who believes in you and encourages you?

If so, when you have the opportunity, give that bright spark of encouragement to someone else.

CHAPTER 16

THE FIRST 59 NOS DON'T APPLY TO YOU

I believe things always work out for the best. I believe every bad decision and every painful moment leads to something good. When people ask, "What would you have done differently?" My answer is always, "Nothing. I needed to learn those lessons."

In the earliest days of our franchise efforts, we were sitting in the call center when someone said, "You know, if we're going to expand into the United States, we need a different phone number than just something local like 738-JUNK. What if we could get an 800 number—what would it be?"

The "Got Milk?" campaign was big in those days, so we thought, "1-800-GOT-JUNK?" And it was like magic, that moment. I said, "Okay, I can see it. Now let's get out there and see who has our phone number."

We dialed 1-800-GOT-JUNK and got a recording saying the number was not in service. So I thought, "Okay, I'm gonna get this phone number." But when I called AT&T, they said the number was definitely being used, but it was activated in only one state. If you called 1-800-GOT-JUNK from outside that state, you'd get a recording that the number was not in service. And, of course, the privacy policies of AT&T prohibited them from telling me who owned that phone number, or even the state in which it was active.

I reached out to friends in states all across the United States and asked them to call 1-800-GOT-JUNK to see if anyone answered. I had made a total of fifty-nine calls, and every one of those calls had ended in the same bad news, "No answer."

Nobody could get through, of course, because the only state where that phone number was active was Idaho, one of the few states in the United States where I didn't know anyone.

Meanwhile, I learned that the person who owned 1-888-GOT-JUNK wanted $100,000 for it, so there's no way that was going to happen. And besides, I knew that 1-800-GOT-JUNK was our phone number.

I knew it.

"I can see this phone number. I can see the 1-800-GOT-JUNK? brand." It was a Painted Picture in my mind.

> **Note Eighteen:** To accomplish the miraculous, attempt the ridiculous.

Using present-tense verbs in our Painted Pictures of the future—speaking of things that haven't happened yet as though they already have—isn't the only ridiculous thing we do.

I was so certain this was our phone number that

I actually hired a design company called Drive Design to create the logo exactly as it is today, blue and green with 1-800-GOT-JUNK? in that big, bold font.

I paid for the logo before I had the phone number.

> **Note Nineteen:** The secret to success is to get started before you are ready.

Let me break this down for you:

- Believing is one thing.
- Saying it out loud is another.
- Writing it down and sharing your Painted Picture with others is magical.
- Taking action in advance—like paying to have a logo designed around a phone number you don't own—gives your confidence a concrete foundation on which you can launch a rocket to the stars.

When that phone number was finally answered, it connected me to the telephone room of the Idaho Department of Transportation.

The government owned my number.

I was on my third call with Michael in the phone room at the Idaho Department of Transportation when I said, "I really need this phone number. It's so important."

Michael—who had told me no twice already—said, "We're using it, but not that much." After a long pause, he said, "It's yours. I'm faxing you the paperwork."

Two days later, that paperwork was completed. Everything was done. The number was mine. I called Michael to thank him and ask if I could take him and his team out for dinner, but he was no longer there.

I never even learned Michael's last name.

I don't know if that number was a parting gift to me on his last day of work, or what.

But I do know this:

Note Twenty: At the moment of commitment, the universe conspires to assist you.

(I already told you that back in Chapter 5, but I wanted you to hear it again.)

CHAPTER 17

I CAN SEE IT. CAN YOU?

It was 2012. Erik Church was managing the business, David St. James was managing the Franchise Partners, and we had a year's supply of radio and TV ads written by the Wizard.

It was time to light the fuse on this rocket.

It was time to double the sales of our Franchise Partners.

It was time to paint another picture.

To create a Painted Picture, all you have to do

is see the future as you want it to be, then paint a word picture of that future and share it with everyone you love and trust.

When our CEO dinner was held in Las Vegas in 2012, I took the mic and asked a roomful of partners wearing Hawaiian shirts to close their eyes, so they could see what I saw.

"You are sitting by the beach, twelve feet from the shore, watching the sun set on the horizon. You feel the warm, inviting Hawaiian breeze. You hear the sounds of celebration all around you—music, shared laughter, the clinking of glasses. You're surrounded by some of your closest friends and family, and you pause to reflect on the pride you're feeling. In every entrepreneur's journey, there is a dream. A dream of what is possible. A vision of what success looks like. You have achieved yours. You have doubled your business...and the journey isn't over..."

And then I read them our new Painted Picture.

PAINTED PICTURE 2016

Aloha! Welcome to the beautiful island of Maui and to our annual CEO dinner. Tonight, March 1, 2017, is an evening we've all been looking forward to. Tonight, I reread our 2016 Painted Picture followed by a toast to every Franchise Partner and your teams, to every member of the Junktion (our headquarters), and to members of our families who have joined us in Hawaii to celebrate turning our vision into our reality.

AN EXCEPTIONAL MILESTONE

We live the 1-800-GOT-JUNK? purpose each and every day: to make the ordinary business of junk removal exceptional.

In 2016, we reached an exceptional new milestone together—system-wide sales of $200 million! Our customers have helped fuel our growth with our pervasive brand dominating virtually every market we service. 1-800-GOT-JUNK? is quickly recognized as a leading household name throughout major metros in the United States, Canada, and Australia.

LEADERSHIP

Together, we have built something much bigger and better than any one of us could have built alone. At

1-800-GOT-JUNK? we take pride in leading the way, in taking the road less traveled, in **winning**. Our growth is guided by three leadership principles: Accountability—to each other and our contributions; Collaboration—working together, harnessing the power within our system; and Innovation—perpetually challenging the status quo.

What a feeling it is to be winning. Most of us have more than doubled our 2011 revenues, dominated our markets, and earned countless awards and accolades for our focused efforts! Our intense commitment to competitive intelligence has allowed us to measure the size and potential of our industry, understand the competitive landscape, and make smart decisions that leave our competition in the dust. We are quickly emerging as a world-class brand recognized not for *what* we do, but for *how* we do it. Our leadership shines—a perfect example: over two-thirds of what we remove is diverted from landfills, making 1-800-GOT-JUNK? not only the world's **largest** junk-removal service, but also the **greenest**.

We lead by thinking big, by seeing the possible and then making it happen, executing with great Focus, Faith, and Effort. We are innovators. We create solutions to common problems using technology to improve every aspect of our business. We have enhanced our customer experience. Customers check online to see how far away their truck is, and they view a picture of the driver and navigator who are about to arrive. We have improved our operating effectiveness with an app that provides operations managers with an instant update on how much junk is in the truck and how much revenue has been collected so far for the day. Our business is now paperless for both Truck Teams and our customers. Our innovation is designed to drive **Engagement**, **Awareness**, and **Customer WOW**!

ENGAGEMENT

Engagement is a simple, yet powerful principle: "It's All About People." We are relentless in our pursuit to find the right people and in our commitment to treat them right.

Winning teams are engaged—switched on! Our teams win awards for top employer and top franchisor. Our partnership is at its strongest point in history with a record level of trust and alignment between Franchise Partners and the Junktion. Franchise Partners are engaged, feel supported every step of the way, and many are involved in a leadership role on the Franchise Advisory Council, on a Department Advisory Panel, by helping to host a conference, or by acting as a Peer Mentor. This is true engagement!

The 1-800-GOT-JUNK? culture is in us and everything we do. We are an enviable organization executing with PIPE (Passion, Integrity, Professionalism, and Empathy). Our accelerating flywheel is propelled faster and faster by our intensely focused, yet fun culture. We are results-driven, only recruiting and retaining people who share our values and our excitement for building something special. Our pride is unmistakable. People are banging down doors to work at 1-800-GOT-JUNK? to be a part of our infectious "Blue Wig Spirit." Our central recruiting and screening system has made it easier and faster for Franchise Partners to find our TOMs (which is what we call our junk haulers, who are the frontline of our business).

AWARENESS

People tell us, "I see your trucks everywhere!" Our remarkable marketing style and happy attitude have generated an unprecedented buzz in the residential and commercial service industry. As we continue to expand worldwide awareness, everyone notices our clean, shiny trucks and our friendly, uniformed drivers who take palpable pride in the 1-800-GOT-JUNK? brand. Franchise Partners smile from ear to ear knowing their TOMs are service-industry role models.

No brand has ever received as much attention from the media. Customers instantly trust our brand because we're the company **Oprah** told them about, and **Ellen**, the *Wall Street Journal*, and *Good Morning America*. We've capitalized on this credibility by integrating our media endorsements into an impactful mass-media campaign. Our broadcast strategy has been consistent, cooperative among syndicates, scientifically executed, and a key part of our two-times growth.

Our biggest competitive advantage is how well we connect with our customers! We tap into the power of our customer data to contact them at just the right time with just the right message, taking our marketing results to new heights. Our innovative use of technology engages our customers with hyperpersonalized marketing that is tailored to their unique needs and triggers.

WOW!

If there was one metric that is responsible for our sustained growth, it's our exceptional Net Promoter Score. With our NPS at record levels, it's clear that our customers **love** 1-800-GOT-JUNK?.

Although 1-800-GOT-JUNK? is international in size, our customers experience highly personalized service. We see every interaction with our customers as an opportunity to **connect** with them—from our "go above and beyond" Sales Center to the Welcome Call, from the Truck Team listening to the initial customer call to our unforgettable follow-up and thank-you call. Our agents and Franchise Partners even send hand-written thank-you cards.

We deliver what we promise. We're committed to our QFAs (Quality Focus Areas): On-Time Service; Up-Front Rates; Clean, Shiny Trucks; and Friendly, Uniformed Drivers. Our customers know we've built something special. They **love** it when our TOMs arrive...ahhh, the **RELIEF**!

SUCCESS

Franchise Partner profitability is the fuel that drives 1-800-GOT-JUNK?. We grow the top line without ever taking our eyes off the bottom line. We know Franchise Partner profitability is the key to our growth and success, and both the Junktion and Franchise Partners continue to reinvest their earnings.

"People don't fail; systems do" is a belief woven tightly into our culture. Our search for missing systems and continuous improvement is vital to keeping us on top. Best practices are documented, shared, and encouraged system-wide.

Success means winning, contributing, being recognized, and having **fun**. We work as a team to paint this picture of a globally admired brand. We support one another in reaching personal goals. We celebrate each milestone along this journey of making the ordinary business of junk removal...**exceptional**.

CHAPTER 18

MISTAKE: I SAID MAUI. WE CELEBRATED ON KAUAI.

Five hundred of us gathered at the Grand Hyatt on Kauai, a truly remarkable place, to live the picture we had painted four years earlier.

It's important to note that some of the things we saw in the Painted Picture haven't happened—yet. We're still waiting for Ellen to invite us for a dance on her show (Ellen, if you're reading this, we're available any time!). But we said we would double the business, and we achieved that—and more.

We're now on trajectory to double again!

Wait. Maybe it's time for a reality check:

> Paul Guy has the highest-volume franchise, but he's in Toronto, a gigantic city.

> A number of partners are beating Paul's performance on a per-capita basis. The size of their towns is their limiting factor.

> But if every 1-800-GOT-JUNK? partner matched Paul's per-capita revenue—keeping in mind that several partners are already exceeding those numbers—1-800-GOT-JUNK? would way exceed its goals.

Okay, reality check over.

We partied like it was 1999. (You remember that Prince song, right?)

Erik Church gave everyone a feeling of stability and confidence.

DSJ electrified the crowd, as he always does. (We promoted him to managing director of 1-800-GOT-JUNK?, by the way.)

The Wizard and his wife, Princess Pennie, joined us to give the partners a glimpse of the newest TV and radio ads.

And of course, I brought the team from the Junktion (our headquarters where all the phone calls are answered), because without them, none of this would have been possible.

CHAPTER 19

ENLARGE YOUR BORDERS

Note Twenty-Two: If you can accomplish your life's work during your lifetime, you're not thinking big enough.

With 1-800-GOT-JUNK? safely in the hands of DSJ, Erik Church and I were free to dream of what could be, might be, should be, will be someday.

Note Twenty-Three: Audacity begins when you start talking about things that haven't happened yet as though they already have. But you must believe in your deepest core that they will come to pass, no matter what.

"We will grow three new franchises, and each of them will be magical."

Like most successful business ideas, all three of our new brands began with a frustration, an experience that was far more tedious than it ought to have been. I said, "Someone ought to..."

And then it hit me, "Why not us?"

I told our head of finance, "We need to start a parent company that will own all our brands."

He said, "What do you want to call it?"

I've always known I'm an ordinary guy.

Ordinary.

And I'm putting together a group of business founders who want to do something exceptional.

Exceptional.

In a flash, our new business name was clear: Ordinary to Exceptional.

That was the moment O2E Brands was born.

PAINT THE
HOUSE

I needed to get my house painted, so I reached out to a handful of friends on Facebook.

Two friends recommended companies I had heard of, so I called both companies and asked for an estimate.

A third friend, one of my favorite people, said, "There's a company called One Day Painting. You should talk to this guy, Jim."

So the first two guys pulled up, and they reeked of cigarette smoke from the moment they walked in the door. They were late, they were disorganized, and they weren't in uniform. I didn't have a good feeling about them.

But then the third guy, Jim Bodden, walked in. He was uniformed. His estimating system was on an iPad, and he had a shiny van outside that read, "One Day Painting." I thought, "Okay, this is good."

Jim said, "My prices are going to be the same as everyone else's, and my quality is going to be excellent. The kicker is that when we agree on a painting day, I'll have your house done that same day."

I said to him, "Are you kidding me?"

He pointed to his van outside and said, "One Day Painting. It's what we do."

"I don't know how that's possible, but okay." And we shook hands. But I was thinking in my mind, "Even if it takes two days, it's a whole lot faster than two weeks."

I booked the painting day and came home at 6:30

that evening. Floor to ceiling, the walls were perfect, as were all the moldings and trim. And the kitchen had needed three coats because of the dark color that had previously been there. It, too, was immaculate. The job was perfect. I was blown away.

I called Jim and raved, "Thank you! Unbelievable! Great service! Have you ever looked at franchising your business?"

He said, "Actually, I've tried. It doesn't work."

I said, "Can we grab a beer and talk? Maybe there's a way I can help."

Then I called James Alisch, an expert in the painting business, and said, "I'm hoping to acquire this company, One Day Painting, and revolutionize the painting space. Let's go for lunch and talk."

At the end of lunch, James said, "Don't do it. Don't acquire this business. It will never work. If you do this, you're freaking nuts."

He gave me a million reasons why it wouldn't work,

but his biggest concern was this: the timeline was too quick to provide a quality painting service.

> **Note Twenty-Four:** When you're told no, you have two choices: let it douse your flame, or use it as fuel to light the fire.

For me, "no" is a powerful motivator to try the impossible. So even though a friend (and painting expert) had called me crazy, I acquired the business and franchised it anyway. It wasn't long before I got a real reality check.

I'll admit, I had been a little bit arrogant when I thought, "We've done this once—we can do it again!"

Two years later, we were in the painting business.

But customers weren't connecting with the concept of One Day Painting. The company wasn't gaining momentum like it should. We couldn't figure it out.

Deep down, I suspected our problem might be that we used Jim Bodden's original logo colors, blue and orange, and they gave us the look and feel of a college football team. This isn't the feeling that people are after when painting their homes.

Have you ever done the right thing in the wrong way? That's what I did. I took the perfect idea, One Day Painting, an idea whose time had come, and dressed it up in clothes that didn't fit it.

Finally, I said, "We have to rebrand."

Do you remember what I said about the universe conspiring to assist you? I was in Florence, Italy, with my family. We were walking along the sidewalk when we saw this wonderful little gelato shop with *fifty* flavors. One of them had a smiley face on top made from half a lime and a couple of little pieces of candy, so I said, "I want that flavor. It's smiling at me. It's talking to me." I immediately took a photo of that gelato and sent it to our logo designer with a text message, "Capture this magic for WOW 1 DAY PAINTING."

He captured that magic, and our company was immediately transformed.

There it was again, that old pattern of failure, success. I had let my arrogance convince me that my systems and my experience could overcome a weak brand image. But I was wrong. Our failure clearly proved it.

But here's the important thing to remember: failure is a temporary condition. We saw our failure, acknowledged that failure, and found a way to correct it. The bright light of creativity shines brightest when you recognize your failure and embrace it with optimism.

I just happened to be looking at gelato in Italy when that bright light suddenly filled my mind.

I showed our new branding package to James Alisch. He said, "I want in."

All it took to transform James from a naysayer to an evangelist was a repackaging of the brand. And that's how James "If-You-Do-This-You're-Freaking-Nuts" Alisch became the managing director of WOW 1 DAY PAINTING.

He's made it so successful that he now manages two of our emerging O2E Brands.

CHAPTER 21

AND NOW IT'S TIME TO MOVE

So now it was time for my wife, Lara, and me to move to a new house.

I had met a guy who came to the Junktion for a tour. He owned a moving company, an old family business. He said, "Hey. If you're ever gonna move, here's my card. I'm your guy. I'll give you the VIP treatment."

I kept the card, and I called him.

One of their branding messages is "Guaranteed on-time arrival."

They were forty-five minutes late.

We had just installed brand-new carpet in the basement, to which they added a dark brown stripe of muddy footprints.

The movers were all wearing earbuds with music blaring. They would shout to me, "Where does this box go?"

So I'd tell them, and they'd shout, "Where? What?"

I wanted to say, "If you took out your earbuds, you'd be able to hear me." But I just smiled and shouted a little louder.

I heard them upstairs saying, "I think we have a problem."

So I went up there, and I said, "How can I help?"

They'd had trouble getting our mattress up the narrow stairwell, so they unzipped the mattress cover and took our organic cotton mattress apart. You know when you make a lasagna and you've got all those layers of noodles and it's a bit of a mess? That was our mattress.

We had to get a new one.

Who unzips a mattress cover and takes the mattress apart?

I mean, it was just one thing after another.

You Move Me was born when they knocked the head off my wife's favorite plant and killed it.

Lara really loved that plant.

I respect people who are able to admit their mistakes, so when the owner of the moving company asked if he could come by and get my feedback, I said, "I'm willing to meet with you, but please know that I'm going to give you the feedback completely straight up. I don't want a discount. I don't want anything at all. But if you really want the feedback, I'm willing to do that for you."

So I told him everything, and then I said, "And I'm

probably going to start a company in this space because I don't think it should be this bad."

He thanked me for being honest with him. "I'm definitely going to make some changes to my business," he said.

Have you ever had an experience and thought, "There must be a better way?" I've learned to listen to my instincts—this is often the best way to spot possibility. You never know where inspiration will strike!

I talked to a group of people I trusted, and we were all energized by the opportunity to shake up the moving space. So Erik Church, Paul Guy, Tom Rypma, Laurie Baggio, and I decided to get together to talk about starting a moving business. We agreed to meet in Vancouver, then head up to Whistler for our meeting.

Tom called and said, "I got bumped to the next flight. I'm gonna be about four hours late."

So Paul said, "Let's go buy tracksuits."

We all looked at him and said, "What?"

"Let's go buy matching tracksuits."

We said, "That sounds ridiculous. So, okay...sure."

We drove into downtown Vancouver and bought five matching tracksuits. Blue Adidas with white stripes down the leg. Matching shoes, matching socks, matching T-shirts. Nothing but blue and white. We got into our white limo and headed to the airport to pick up Tom.

Tom walked out of the baggage claim and saw we were all in matching tracksuits. "Where's mine?"

We handed him his tracksuit. "Go into the bathroom and put it on. We're here to talk about creating a moving business."

Tom said, "Why tracksuits?"

Paul said, "Why not?

Note Twenty-Five: Take your business seriously, but never take yourself too seriously.

We spent two days in Whistler in matching Adidas tracksuits, envisioning the perfect moving experience, and figuring out how to deliver it.

At the end of those two days in Whistler, we were pumped. We immediately contacted all the 1-800-GOT-JUNK? partners, and twenty-five of them instantly bought the You Move Me franchise rights for their areas.

I had been told by an expert not to do this, but hey, I knew better, right?

More than half of those initial Franchise Partners ended up throwing in the towel and giving up their territories only a couple of years in.

Wait a second: How many times do I need to make this mistake before I finally realize that I'm not as different as I think I am?

Looking back, I now realize that some of those 1-800-GOT-JUNK? Franchise Partners weren't as hungry or as hands-on as they used to be. The simple truth is they were living the good life and didn't want to work that hard anymore. They weren't thinking like founders when they bought into You Move Me. They were thinking like investors.

But that wasn't true of all of them. Tyler and Josh were doing millions each year in Kansas City before anyone knew what was happening. And now dozens of other happy, hungry, hardworking, hands-on founders are following their lead and performing magnificently as well.

Thanks for your leadership as founders, Tyler and Josh!

But let's be clear about this: Lara is still annoyed about that plant.

And I'm still passionate about figuring out how to reinvent the moving industry.

CHAPTER 22

CLEAN THE GUTTERS

Rain was gushing down the side of the house so that every time you walked outside you got soaking wet. My wife, Lara, said, "You've got to get those gutters cleaned."

So I went online and began calling people who said they cleaned gutters, but they weren't returning my phone calls. I left messages. I sent emails. But not a single person got back to me. Zero. I literally got no response from any of the companies on Google or Craigslist.

I was telling my story to Leigh Adler, a WOW 1

DAY PAINTING Franchise Partner. "I can't find anyone to clean my gutters. It's driving me nuts."

Leigh said, "Call Igor. He's working with a guy named Dave Notte to build up a thing called Shack Shine."

I said, "Dave Notte? I know Dave Notte."

Dave was another College Pro Painters friend of Paul Guy. Twenty years earlier, Dave had approached me to buy the 1-800-GOT-JUNK? franchise in Vancouver, but I wouldn't sell it to him, because I wasn't quite ready to get out of the junk-removal business and go 100 percent into the franchise business. So, Dave launched a big commercial painting business, and built a multimillion-dollar business.

Igor and Dave came by to look at my gutters. We had a mildly amusing moment when I walked outside and found them having a prep meeting about how they were going to impress me.

I learned a few days later that they really wanted to land this job because Dave had a much bigger agenda than just cleaning my gutters.

Shack Shine cleaned my gutters, and I was blown away by the service. It was thorough, it was quick, it was great.

Dave sent me an email and asked, "So, how was it?"

I replied, "Awesome. It was completely awesome."

He said, "I think Shack Shine should be part of O2E Brands."

And I'm like, "Oh, really?"

He said, "About a year ago, I said to myself, 'Brian Scudamore walked into a fragmented industry, a dirty, nonglamorous business that nobody loved, and he built it into an empire. What can I create like that?'"

Still stinging from the brand-image mistake I made with WOW 1 DAY PAINTING and limping from the shortcut I took with You Move Me, I didn't feel quite ready for another new brand. But Dave was persistent and kept after me. About once a quarter, we would get together and have lunch and talk about it.

Then one day, I acquired it.

I kept the Shack Shine name, which I liked, but I didn't like the logo. So I went back to Noel Fox, who crafted the WOW 1 DAY PAINTING logo from the gelato photograph I had sent him from Italy.

Noel is my brand of crazy. He understands how to use shapes, colors, font choices, and images to convey exactly what they need to say.

With the help of Dave Notte and Noel Fox and a long list of local partners who are ridiculously happy, hungry, hardworking, and hands-on, Shack Shine quickly became magical. The partners are doing fantastic.

I'm hoping that I finally learned my lesson about arrogance and overconfidence, but every time I start feeling that way, I worry I'm being arrogant and overconfident.

And I think maybe that's a healthy thing.

CHAPTER 23

THE PURPOSE OF HEROES

Tell me what a person admires, and I'll tell you everything about them that matters.

What do you admire?

I admire the personal discipline and organization of my father.

I admire the courage and encouragement of my mother.

I admire the way my grandparents treated people.

And I admire my third-grade teacher, Mr. Dodds.

Mr. Dodds never said, "Don't do this. Don't do that. You can't be this." He just made you feel accepted. He went out of his way to involve me in things he knew I had a talent for. He would play floor hockey with us when he volunteered after school. I never felt a sense of judgment from him for anything, ever. He accepted you just like you were; how you were and who you were was fine with him.

The culture of O2E Brands is that we accept everyone just as they are, like Mr. Dodds. We treat them with respect, like my grandparents. We encourage them, like my mother. And we have the professional discipline and high level of organization like my father.

These people are my heroes.

Who are yours?

Grandpa Kenny passed away in 1987, when I was in eleventh grade. I know that if he'd passed away just two years later, when I had finished high school, I would have taken over the army surplus business. But the timing didn't work out that way, and Grandma Florence didn't want to run it on her own, so she shut it down.

But I learned about business from them.

I was inspired by them.

I saw how much fun they had.

I would have been perfectly happy running Lorber's Surplus, but the universe had other plans.

> **Note Twenty-Six:** When a door closes in your face, don't be disappointed. Everything is going to be all right in the end.

If things aren't all right, it's not the end.

Again, who are your heroes?

Here's why it's important for you to know the answer to that question.

We have historic heroes, business heroes, folk heroes, and comic-book heroes. We have heroes in books, songs, movies, and sports. We have heroes of leadership, heroes of excellence, and heroes of kindness.

And nothing is so devastating to our sense of well-being as a badly fallen hero.

Heroes are dangerous to have.

The only thing more dangerous is not to have them.

Heroes raise the bar we jump and hold high the standards we live by. Our heroes embody all that we're striving to be. We choose our heroes according to our hopes and dreams. And then we create ourselves in their own image.

Myles Reville is a Shack Shine partner in central Toronto, and one of his heroes is Paul Guy.

Here's how it happened.

I was connecting with some ex-College Pro Painters guys, and Myles was one of them. I sent him a message through LinkedIn, and he fired me back a message saying, "Hey, it's funny you sent me a message. I'm looking out the window of my apartment right now at the signs above your Toronto office."

He appreciated that it was serendipitous and weird that I sent him a message while he was looking at our signs. We chatted a bit. He said he had just arrived in Toronto and was looking to do something new, so I connected him to our Shack Shine team, and Myles became a partner.

Myles Reville ordered his first Shack Shine van and had it shipped to Vancouver—not Toronto—so he could drive it across the continent and recreate Paul Guy's trip. I'm sure you're thinking the same thing I did: "How does that make any sense?"

But Myles said, "If that's how Paul started, I want to start that way, too."

Myles Reville has the heart of a founder. He found a way to make Shack Shine his company, not mine. And he found a way to make Toronto his town. Myles did it by reenacting a historic point of inflection with a road trip to mark that moment he left the past behind and plunged headlong into the future. A road trip that said, "I'm all in. No safety net. My only option is to succeed. No turning back."

Brian Scudamore didn't build 1-800-GOT-JUNK? in Toronto. Paul Guy did. Brian Scudamore didn't build 1-800-GOT-JUNK? in San Francisco. Tom Rypma did. And I didn't build 1-800-GOT-JUNK? in Seattle. Nick Wood and his tattoo did. The success these partners achieved is their own success. It wasn't purchased. It was earned.

The same is true of all our partners. This is what it means to have the heart of a founder.

I provide the blueprints and the tools, but our partners choose the town and build the house. And to build a house worth owning, you must have the heart of a founder, not of an investor.

The blueprints I give them are time-tested systems, policies, and procedures. The tools are technology and marketing and a brand that people love. A founder takes those blueprints in one hand and swings a hammer with the other.

No one can sell you success. It has to be earned.

Blue wigs, bowling shirts, temporary tattoos (and permanent ones), Adidas tracksuits, and inexplicable cross-country road trips are just some of the ways our happy tribe of founders shout, "I'm loving living life!"

Every morning when I wake up, I'm incredibly thankful that I didn't sell the company to Waste Management when they asked. If I had, I would never have met all these happy, wonderful people who have gotten excited about entrepreneurship. But it's not a money thing. Each of us is similar in that we like to be needed, we like making people happy, and we like to be part of something that's growing and fun.

> **Note Twenty-Seven:** The key to daily happiness is to maintain an attitude of gratitude.

I believe we live in a world where people are driven too much by money.

Money seems, to me, to be a by-product rather than a goal. Money flows to you of its own accord when you do the right things, in the right ways, at the right time.

That momentary feeling of success you get because of the car you're driving, or the house you're living in, never lasts for long. The happiest people I know are those for whom money isn't even near the top of their list. They're choosing purpose, lifestyle, family, friends, fun—things that money can never buy.

I believe if people stopped talking so much about getting rich, and just appreciated the riches they already have in their lives, they'd be a lot happier.

THE BIGGER THE SETBACK, THE GREATER THE COMEBACK

To succeed without ever failing would be a hollow victory. Deep in your heart, you would always know you didn't earn it.

But if you can tell riveting stories of disappointment and regret and longing and refusing to give up—even when giving up would have made more sense—well, you deserve everything you've achieved.

You are going to embrace your mistakes with a smile. That's why you're going to succeed beyond anyone's expectations.

I know it.

You know it.

Your mentor will know it.

And your family and friends will definitely know it.

Is there anybody else who really matters? If there is, they'll know it, too.

As we bring our time together to a close, here are ten things I hope you'll remember:

1. Failure is the key that unlocks the door to true success; its value is that it teaches you what you need to know. Never be afraid to try, fail, and learn.

2. Failure is a temporary condition; interestingly, so is success.

3. The only way to reduce the number of failures you must endure is to embrace a worthy mentor who will let you learn from his or her failures.

4. Keep in mind that after you've chosen your worthy mentor, your mentor must also choose you.

5. Surround yourself with passionate people who think and act like founders.

6. If every person in your organization leads people smaller than themselves, you will become a company of tiny people.

7. If every person in your organization leads people greater than themselves, you will become a company of giants.

8. Choose your heroes wisely. In the end, they define you.

9. True happiness is to enjoy the present without fear about the future.

10. Be WTF (Willing to Fail!).

There's a difference between making a living and making a life.

I hope you have as much fun making a life as I do.

CHAPTER 25

YOUR STORY

From this day on, your future is a blank slate.
What's the story you'll be telling?